How to *Feel* and *Understand*

Love Attraction

How to Feel and Understand Love Attraction

Love Attraction

Kat Kem M

BALBOA.
PRESS
A DIVISION OF HAY HOUSE

ISBN: 978-1-4525-5150-0 (sc)
ISBN: 978-1-4525-5151-7 (e)

Library of Congress Control Number: 2012907984

Balboa Press books may be ordered through booksellers or by contacting:

Balboa Press
A Division of Hay House
1663 Liberty Drive
Bloomington, IN 47403
www.balboapress.com
1-(877) 407-4847

Because of the dynamic nature of the Internet, any web addresses or links contained in this book may have changed since publication and may no longer be valid. The views expressed in this work are solely those of the author and do not necessarily reflect the views of the publisher, and the publisher hereby disclaims any responsibility for them.

The author of this book does not dispense medical advice or prescribe the use of any technique as a form of treatment for physical, emotional, or medical problems without the advice of a physician, either directly or indirectly. The intent of the author is only to offer information of a general nature to help you in your quest for emotional and spiritual well-being. In the event you use any of the information in this book for yourself, which is your constitutional right, the author and the publisher assume no responsibility for your actions.

Any people depicted in stock imagery provided by Thinkstock are models, and such images are being used for illustrative purposes only. Certain stock imagery © Thinkstock.

Printed in the United States of America

Balboa Press rev. date:5/18/2012

How to Feel and Understand Love Attraction
by Kat Kemm

Dedicated to all my teachers, including my children, friends, friends of my children, spouses, my parents, and those who have passed briefly by my life to share love on many levels.

Contents

Preface

We have lost our way in love. We have forgotten to look at our ancestors and how they related intimately in love relationships to each other. We have forgotten to include our souls in the process of love. I pray my own work and process with understanding love helps humanity in its forward movement to receive, blend, and balance all the energies of the feminine aspect of love. The feeling center of the heart equals the feminine aspect of love.

Introduction

Love brings a warm feeling of peace that each of us seeks. With love comes acceptance and comfortable being. Love propels forward movement in the human race. Finding love, keeping love, being in love, having an open heart, and not feeling dead within is the movement forward.

Love is the feeling of belonging, acceptance, peace, a knowing all is well, contentment, a place of relaxation, a place of feeling safe, a place of giving and receiving, a place of rest, and a place where we feel close to God.

Love is the magical feeling of warm contentment where movement can flow with the colors of the seen world and movement of goodness in the unseen world, where all good happens and nurtures the soul of mankind. The unseen world of goodness moves through love, through the prayer of acceptance, through the prayer of forgiveness, through the prayer of nurturing by giving and service, through the acceptance of listening, and through the gift of time. Love makes it possible to heal the wounds of all time, both past and present.

The feeling of love brings two souls together, so each has a space to evolve to a higher level of consciousness. Two souls coming together in agreement brings the entire human population up a notch in conscious listening. A fresh wind of love will move a person stuck in the mud to generate forward movement to what has not shown itself in present time.

To bring the souls together, there will be forces of attraction through eros (discussed in chapter 3), karmic love (discussed in chapter 4), marriage or union (discussed in chapter 11), romantic love, sacred love (discussed in chapter 2), and spiritual love. These types of love are generated by influences of the mirror, love wounds, love healing, love avoiders, self love, soul love, lineage clearing, and invisible forces working to the greater good.

You are about to venture upon your own self-reflection, your own identification, and an examination of how you relate to love. You will learn about karmic love, how the love wound begins, and love healing. Key insights into love and why we attract others into our life through love are in coming chapters.

By the time you finish reading this book, you will be able to identify what draws and attracts you to emotional love, ideal love, karmic love, sacred love, romantic love, or true love. In the end, you will find all love relationships are our best teachers, and that there are no regrets with love.

CHAPTER 1

Divine Feminine

Male role modeling has been going on for thousands of years and has been very much instilled in our psyche and lineage for generations. We need only to read our history books to remind us. Positive male role modeling has been the leader and innovator. Negative male role modeling has been the warrior and the aggressor.

The *divine feminine* is the blending of the feminine and the masculine. Combining the forces of receptivity and intuition in harmony and balance with leadership strength creates the divine feminine. The concept of right versus wrong is not valid here. The duality of good versus bad does not exist. Give and take is the concept. Honoring, allowing, and receiving create the force.

Shedding the skin of rigidity, control, and misunderstanding from masculine role model in favor of compassion and empathy from the feminine role model creates harmony, balance, and peace.

The wound of the feminine is deep within and difficult to overcome; yet confronting the wound to clear it of abandonment and non-nurturing will heal it for the whole. The deep wound caused by nurturing and empathy is absent in the first love relationship. Many therapists and trained professionals receive their income because of the existence of this wound.

Look to the earth as our example of the feminine. She takes abuse beyond human measure, yet she gives freely. By giving water and support beneath our feet, she nurtures all of humanity. Once in a while, she will gurgle and burp. She will hiccup an earthquake or move with a shift. Father sky will come tickle her with the wind. The love affair between earth and sky is the balance humanity seeks in living daily lives.

In looking at the earth, the feminine, there is solidarity—grounded, available, intuitive, compassion. The sky, the masculine, is bossy, take-charge, controlling, moody, flighty, good one day, naughty the next, and unpredictable. Putting these analogies side by side, we begin to see how the wound came to be.

The air expects the earth to always be there, to always be receptive and nurturing, when the feminine is having her moment to be within herself—like air always does. The wound occurs when the air does something hurtful such as producing a big wind, a hurricane, a tornado, or a massive destructive heat wave, throwing nature out of balance and into chaos.

How does humanity move between the patriarchal and matriarchal to combine the two into balance, becoming the divine feminine? We shift the balance through relationships, and by sharing love with one another in deep, intimate connections. The mirror reflection of a relationship shows who we are to ourselves. The mirror reflection also reveals old emotions needing to be released, so new emotions of love can come through. For instance, a widow, having a casual friendship with another person who has experienced spousal abandonment, can bring up feelings of repressed grief even though that spouse has not physically died.

The balance comes from doing the inner work and action in the physical world.

Much of your work will require going within yourself to resolve issues of the past—including even your lineage and ancestry. Many people already do this, allowing laws of forgiveness, commitment, gratitude, and anything that sparks feelings of love to rule the day.

As our heart center opens by facing emotional and soul wounds, we release behavior patterns and go from feeling isolated, alone and like the only person on the planet to feel as we do, to feeling love, acceptance and balance within.

Consciously, we trudge through the mud and sludge of old emotions that hold us back from living on a higher plane of acceptance and thought. Our life then becomes the prayer of sacred love, global love, spiritual love, sacred partnership, and the feeling of romantic love forever.

When you meet someone who seems magical, the feeling you experience exists because that person appears to emanate huge amounts of divine light. The divine feminine energy is compassionate to all forms of life. Look to the earth to understand the feminine. Standing barefoot on her will relax your inner being.

The moon, too, is feminine. The moon mirrors our emotions. A full moon often inspires a high level of romance and eroticism. The lover, emanating emotions, from the moon shows the power of attraction, sensuality, and desire. Full moon phases can stimulate a powerful desire to find a soul mate and a drive to make that connection. The seed of all relationships is love, whether eros or karmic love gets you together. Divine, compassionate love is the love that heals and does not judge, prosecute, or ignore.

CHAPTER 2

Sacred Love

Human nature does not tolerate another person ruling over us by commanding, controlling, and directing service from us. *Sacred love* is service. The service of sacred love is not controlled by ego but by the heart. The heart allows us to serve our community, family, humanity, and ourselves. Sacred love involves stepping beyond yourself, the person you created in your own mind, to offer yourself to another for that person's healing and growth. This service is required for sacred love to grow.

Putting sacred love into daily practice requires acknowledgement that each person is a part of the greater whole of humanity. It involves knowing the feminine principles of balance, sharing, and harmony, and understanding our powerlessness over another. We must know that our own nurturing is the responsibility of thoughts, actions, and behaviors. The feminine practice of nurturing others extends to the practice of nurturing self in preference to others. This nurturing of self serves the greater whole in the cosmic puzzle.

Whether sacred love comes from serving a family or having a job outside the home, all actions feed and water the growth of each soul in the cog of humanity's wheel of forward movement. Through service, we let go and allow the unseen world of the invisible forces of good to weave a trail of goodness and calm.

Sacred love is about the feminine principle of divine equity. Service to self and others at the same time produces divine equity, which also balances the scales of feminine and masculine. Sacred love means remaining an eagle in flight, with fierce love and focus on that which allows the soul to spread out and fly.

Anything or anyone that does not make the soul come alive will not serve in this sacred love of partnership with the divine feminine—being in the center of heart feeling, feeling the soul speaking truth through the heart. The mind, master of masculinity, is not the master here. The heart of love, the feeling center of the feminine, is the focus of the beating drum drumming on life.

Meditation

Imagine: high up in the cosmos is a beautiful white light coming straight down through the top of your head, all the way through your feet, to the center of the earth, and then back up through your body to the cosmos. Feel this while visualizing your entire body surrounded by a geometric shape that spins while the white light is coursing through your body to the center of the earth. You can do this anytime and anywhere. Visualize the light passing through others while watching their amazing transformation into a state of peace and relaxation.

About Sacred Love

Sacred love does not require you to be a doormat! Sacred love requires you to remain an eagle of fierce love and focus in flight. In a partnership, you must have the liberty to express yourself freely. You must be available to your inner desires and not abandon your inner personality.

You must not surrender to overpowering masculine energies. Be a sharing female. Be a female of harmony. Stay fierce in your focus on these energies while you fly.

Act as a landlady who has been renting space to male energies that no longer serve. Anything that does not make you come alive does not serve anymore.

A non-functioning, discounting relationship will not survive sacred love. Since sacred love is all about service, anyone who is non-functioning creates chaos and distractions, thereby negating service to anyone. The relationship and the person perpetuating these male energies will fall away. Your own vibration will be such that your level of toleration will be unsustainable.

The male energies of control and rigidity will not hold. Only the feminine energies will hold and carry forward through these coming years of growth and prosperity. Nothing and no one will hold sway over you. Their vibration does not match your feminine vibration and they will go away.

Abuse

Abuse is the act of discounting and disrespecting the person you are. Abuse results in an energetic block between you and the blocker or controller doing the abusing. Abuse is very old energy, very masculine, and, of course, is unloving. Abuse is non-nurturing. Abuse strips the inner core from a person. Abuse causes parts of your soul to disengage and flee to a place where they can stay until those parts of your soul heal, and you can call all parts of your soul back into your body.

All of us are shedding effects of abuse, tyrannical abuse of power, and the masculine bombardment of ownership through all generations of time.

Abuse of humans began long, long ago, originating in fear. Fear is masculine energy that is dissolving, an energy that will not remain over humanity in our next generations of living. An abusive person has unresolved fears caused by a love wound from early years or past lives in other incarnations.

Feminine energy reflects back to the masculine because of receptivity and mirror effect. The masculine seeing the energy of anger, fear, control, and working from a place of unconscious thought, lashes out at the feminine, causing the abuse. The mirror effect is illumination within.

The chaos created through abuse causes blocks to both parties, resulting in the loss of power and seeing within each inner reality. The landscape becomes muddled and cloudy, thereby causing confusion.

The idea of sacred love and abuse is for the female to remain standing in her power, and to continue to nurture herself, not abandoning her inner self. During these times of shifting from masculine to feminine, the abuse received will reverse itself to one of giving and receiving.

CHAPTER 3

Eros

*E*ros opens the heart. It is driven by passion and that which is erotic. Erotic visions encompass this love. Erotic love feels peaceful. The vibration this love brings through the body is heart-opening, heart-surrendering, and heart-accepting. Visions of being together physically drive this union.

With erotic love, the mirror comes into play as partner. Each participant is in love with what he or she sees and feels through the mirror. This love can become addictive. Not all unions from eros love are addictive. But if each person involved takes steps to connect with the other consciously, the union will flow, and growth will be possible rather than entrapment. Enjoyment by each one contributing to the pleasant feelings this relationship brings will open the heart and release any unstuck places within.

The mirror brings us face-to-face with love wounds that are ready to be released. Embedded deep within the wound of love is extreme loneliness. The person mirroring back always has a similar background and processes of emotions within his or her own love wound. Since erotic love feels so good and is powerful in its intense, stimulating energy, it drives each partner to the other with force that will be impossible to ignore.

Erotic love requires both partners to maintain a balance between the romantic dream and reality. This love emphasizes style, beauty, and romance. The erotic feeling encompasses qualities of sensuous affection, natural courtesy and kindness. The high feeling of peace and gentleness this love brings will open the heart in a way that can be confusing to either partner.

Partners have to listen to their own heart centers and higher selves to perceive what direction the relationship will move after the initial attraction and connection is achieved. Be careful not to push the relationship into the entrapment of marital commitment before old emotional energies of jealousy and ownership have been moved. Otherwise, they will be brought forward and will block the forward movement of each person. If the intensity of attraction slackens, it is possible to recapture the intense feeling so each person feels in love. But this behavior can also backfire badly and create mistrust.

Because we are spiritual beings in physical bodies, we need to feel love in order to raise our vibration. Raising our vibration of acceptance and love while in partnership with another can create conflict, especially if one partner wants to remain in the material world. Conflict does not mean the end of the relationship, but provides an opportunity to open old wounds. Raise our vibration by eating more organic raw fruits and vegetables, drinking pure water, listening to uplifting music, thinking positive thoughts, walking in nature, relaxing in water, reading inspirational books, playing, laughing, and anything that opens our hearts and fills us with joy.

Tapping into old wounds challenges couples to find creative ways to face the process of transformation.

Erotic love must allow partners to air ordinary, day-to-day grievances, pains, annoyances, and human needs. If these ideals are not communicated, then one or both partners may begin to feel deeply unappreciated. The dilemma with a partnership centered upon erotic feeling is that if both partners do not constantly feed the feeling, it has an unpleasant way of transferring itself elsewhere.

The alchemy of the relationship happens when both partners are changed by the energy arising between them. Some of the effects may feel positive, and others may feel deeply disturbing because of inner, ingrained and taught mind images of what it is to be a man or a woman.

CHAPTER 4

Karmic Love

The feeling of *karmic love* is an instant knowing, as if you have met before. The feeling is that the person you have met is "the one." The meeting is so powerful, so consuming, and so intense, that jumping right in feels completely natural. At first the feeling is a floating on air in romantic bliss, everything is perfect, and feels divine. The knowing is that somehow you and your partner must be together. The feeling is in your soul. It is a deep, painful longing, a longing no others can understand unless they, too, have met the same way.

Karmic love is a dangerous love, and not necessarily violent or abusive, but a type of relationship that causes internal fear. This love is consuming, passionate, and frightening. Karmic love relationships often happen when two people come together to heal and evolve as individuals. The lovers meet again to clear negative karma and to rekindle their love. A great deal can be learned from karmic love relationships.

All karmic love relationships are emotionally intense. The lessons learned will be deep and personal, and demand inner strength. One benefit of karmic love relationships is the opportunity they provide to advance your personal evolution through the dynamics of the relationship. The relationship is a gift and a reward, an opportunity to tap into the God-self of the individual person. Since each person is familiar to the other, and the feeling is easy between them, opening their hearts feels easier to them.

Some long-term gains of staying in a karmic relationship are communication, clearing out misunderstandings, dependencies, compulsions, and choices. All are key to making this relationship balanced and whole. Karmic relationships allow each person to open up, allowing them to discuss the condition of their souls, ridding their minds of secrets and illusions.

The ego is a distraction in dealing with karmic relationships because problems of the soul feeling vulnerable and raw are unpleasant and uncomfortable. Power issues are involved here. Tensions arise when the dependent in the relationship takes back their power previously given up in order to be in the relationship. One must stay open to evolve and forgive.

If you ride the waves of the relationship as though you are a ship that is safe and protected, then reacting with fear will lessen, and love will bloom. Your efforts will lead you toward feeling happy and working harmoniously.

We establish a karmic relationship because unconsciously we see in another person something that can effectively help us solve some of our limitations, thereby opening up our soul. Not all karmic relationships have to be demanding and complicated. Upon deciding to become conscious by choosing, we transform mindful, behavior negative patterns. Intentions, which are a form of prayer and thought, have the alchemy of growing strength and awareness in our lives.

The intention of karmic relationships is to heal the love wound and bring up issues of the shadow within. All relationships, whether intimate or friendships, have some sort of mirror effect. Through relationships, the mirrors reflect our true selves, within which we cannot see.

Jesus irritated many people because his truth sowed light on their darkness. Yet without the light shining on the darkness, the dark will not be seen. Light is necessary for dark and the dark is the wound, the hidden, the shamed part of ourselves we want to keep in the shadows, to deny and run from. By not facing the dark, we wither away, our soul disconnects, and we numb ourselves to reality through various forms, thereby giving our power away.

We are pushed to heal love wounds received from our ancestors, so future generations walk forth and prosper the earth. The future generations become the nurturing, the loving, healing people.

CHAPTER 5

Love Healing

Healing the love wound is a process. We call into our lives other souls to confront the wound. Sometimes we listen. Sometimes we choose not to listen by running away or using any number of escapes to numb the pain from the wound. Sometimes we don't wake up until the next time around, in another body.

Earth presents harsh realities to persons confronting the Divine within. Relationships, and especially love relationships, are most effective in confronting the wound. That wound began when our souls separated from the Divine to come into a body.

The idea behind love healing is to use the negative vibrations of relationship to confront our own inner selves. As humans, our linear brains talk our souls down. Our programming from our family of origin takes over. We become walking, talking humans, with a brain that we feed, and a heart center, which is aligned with the soul that we ignore because of the brain and its logic.

We have to confront the beginnings of the wound while conscious because the wound we are operating from causes us to work in the subconscious. Sometimes going back in time to look at our lineage and how our ancestors related to each other in the context of intimacy will release negative feelings attached to the wound.

If the DNA in the lineage of women evokes a feeling of low worth, and this feeling carries through each generation of women, then that feeling of low worth started with the original separation from God and compounded with her human relationships on earth. The wound was miniscule when the soul left God to come into the body, but somehow, through the brain programming and passing it down through the generations of women, low self-worth built upon itself in each generation. This is why lineage clearing is so important: to clear out that old language, to go back to each female in every generation and forgive them for not stepping into their power and starting their generation fresh. For a man to clear out old language is to go through every generation where men misused power over women.

The Transition of Soul

The soul comes into the body whole, with a slight trauma from leaving the divine station. The soul carries the memory of the separation from the Divine.

The soul experiences abandonment or trauma pain from the parental relationship while in a body. The brain at an infant stage can process only so much with limited training. During these phases of parental or family trauma, the soul is capable of splitting off outside of the body. Not the entire soul, but parts of the soul split off. The pain hurts. The soul that split off wants to return to the Divine, where all things are safe, comfortable, and nourishing.

We continue on as people living our lives, unconscious that our entire soul is not in our body and bring into our lives romantic love relationships to heal the split off part of the soul. We have to call all parts of our soul back into the body to fully function with wholeness in the love relationship.

Meditation for Calling the Soul Back

You are sitting in the middle of the front row in a theatre. As you look around, notice what animal shows up and is sitting around you and behind you. These are your animal medicine guides.

As you tune into your animal medicine guides, tell them you call all parts of your soul back now. All parts of your soul are fully healed. You will see them run off and pick up the lost pieces of your soul and bring them right in, either through your crown—the top of your head—or your heart center. After the parts of your soul have been retrieved and are safely returned, say, "All parts of my soul are back, fully healed, fully functioning, and may my soul harm none." Thank your medicine animals and journal.

These putting-the-soul-back-in-the-body and soul-retrieval sessions are not painful, but leave a person with feelings of peace, wholeness, and confidence. Several sessions may be necessary.

Addiction

People with addictions have soul loss. People in ongoing active addictions have tremendous disconnection from themselves and their souls. Twelve-step programs really work at putting the soul back through many years of going to meetings and staying sober. All wounds that lead to addiction start in non-nurturing environments that become manifest in adulthood.

A type of addiction that is silent is the love addiction where one person obsesses about the other and the other is a love avoider. Usually the love avoider comes back and forth in the relationship, gets the hit from admiration, and leaves through emotional disconnection. Love addiction relationships run a course of intensity in due time. When this happens, we are left feeling heartbreak and extreme loss of time spent. We feel traumatized and misunderstood.

Addiction in all forms has to do with obsession and preoccupation. Sex addiction is a big hidden addiction within society today. The cerebral male uses sex to feel. Sexually addicted persons connect with passion and intensity, but disconnect as fast as they connect. This on-and-off connection creates a longing within the other person. Sex addicts come in and go out of your life, but do not stay the entire time. At some point, disconnection happens because maintaining intensity is impossible. This connection and disconnection creates within the feeling of abandonment.

There are other types of love addicts: battered, abusive, anorexic, romantic, and avoidant love addicts. The love avoider is very rigid or compulsive. For the love avoider there is no in between. It's either, "I want you," or, "No, I don't want you." The love avoider pulls you in and pushes you away. The love avoider feels empowered when creating this push-pull dynamic with love because it creates chaos and needing of the other person to worship him, which is a fix. Once the fix of being needed and worshipped is met, the love avoider pulls away to start the tension all over again. Chaos results.

In relationship to the love avoider, the other person, usually the female, must remain the eagle in flight, staying focused on her own life. She should seek out things that spark her own feelings of love and that allow her own wings to spread out and fly.

Something to remember when entering or maintaining a relationship is that loss of self is painful. Staying in a relationship to maintain security means giving up your power. Eventually, parts of your soul will leave. When that happens, you become disempowered, and the dark side of the hidden realm steps in.

To feel safe and get on track with what love really means is to return to the divine feminine, embodying both masculine and feminine. The sacred marriage is where we heal ourselves within. We do not abandon ourselves. We see ourselves as staying in the flow, and know that we are done serving ego, but serve only spirit, source, or God.

CHAPTER 6

Understanding the Inner Feminine

(by Being the High Priestess and Queen)

Being in touch with the inner feminine is more complicated than it appears to be! The model for the true power of femininity has been lost over recent history and is now becoming re-energized through the acceptance of feminine archetypes. The high priestess, through her intuition, and the queen role model, through her leadership, express these feminine archetypes. Recovering this feminine power is a personal task for each woman and man. This process is the starting point for self-healing and provides the essence of personal security.

The primary energies associated with the inner feminine are the moon and the planet Venus. The moon is the energy filtering through the subconscious self and tells the story of connection to the part providing nurturing, support, care, and comfort. The person who modeled the moon is the mother, and you see her through the lens of your own emotional matrix, signified by the moon. As adults mature, they learn to send this energy out into the world, but to be truly effective you must first own this energy and know how to use it to care for yourself!

Look into your astrological chart to determine what moon you were born under, and you will see the feminine archetypes associated with this moon and the energies you are to send out into the world. The moon's feminine archetypes are addressed in the next chapter.

Everything feminine is elevated. The feminine love energy is all about inclusive, connecting partnerships, and about compassion, communion, commitment, and consistency in relationships. We are learning to communicate the feminine energy as a whole. Some males, have struggles accepting the shift. Their world as they know it, through control and manipulation, is not working anymore and is collapsing fast. Wives are saying, "No more," and are walking away. Girlfriends are speaking truth, are no longer supporting the male patriarchal behavior, and will not support it for a long time to come. The feminine energy is rising and will be the way again.

Religions were created and built during patriarchal reign. Then pagan practices were suppressed but not forgotten. Pagan practices, which are the feminine energy, are the same as nature: the earth. Everything related to the earth is feminine. We walk in nature and begin to feel divine presence, or receive a message about a problem we are dealing with. We trust and are open while in nature.

The feminine honors intuition; it honors mother earth. We look to the mother—our earth—to find the feminine and how we relate to each other with the feminine caring energy of love. The mother earth—our supporter, nurturer, and lover of humanity—holds space for us through the ages of time.

Each of us is a transmitter for the moon sign we were born under, and we are shifting consciously as we embrace these energies in becoming a conscious participant. No matter which gender you are expressing you will yield to the more feminine expression of yourself. The feminine in you, the emotionally intuitive, the mystic and telepathic communicator, is evolving forth. When we learn to pull the emotional nature out of relationship dramas from negativity and despair to ecstasy, creativity, and intuition, the faster we will shift into the feminine energy of acceptance and love.

Honoring the intuitive feeling mind as the sacred feminine gift is the energy we are walking into, rather than listening to the rational mind, which is associated with male patriarchal energy. Another factor of your moon energy goes beyond your deepest needs and shows what they are. You can feel whole only when these needs are answered and fulfilled. Although it is tempting to look outside, your wisdom tells you that a great part of the responsibility for nourishment comes from within yourself.

CHAPTER 7

Moon Signs, Feminine Traits, and Archetypes

Aries Moon—Fire energy is associated with sending out will through courage. An Aries has the ability to face danger without being overcome by fear. Aries's feminine archetypes are damsel, intuitive, survivor, advocate, and leader. An Aries can also have traits of playfulness or impulsiveness, and is easily excited.

Taurus Moon—The calm in the center of the storm. Taurus's feminine archetypes are Venus (Aphrodite), the goddess, the creator, artist, musician, sensualist, the lover who is patient and secure. Taurus is a feminine sign; in a crisis Tauruses may retreat. They love good food and being surrounded by beauty. All Taurus's feminine archetypes relate to how our mother earth responds to humanity.

Gemini Moon—Can step into magic through shape-shifting by mutating into whoever is in the room. Gemini's feminine archetypes are a storyteller, a guide, a student, a teacher, a child, a gossip, or a socialite. Geminis have to let go of sadness and rage to step into their feeling center. They can have an angel's or a devil's personality. Some feminine traits they embrace are variety, freedom, and change.

Cancer Moon—The natural feminine. Cancers relate to home, hearth, family, and feelings. All they want is love and appreciation—which is exactly what our mother the earth, wants. Their feminine archetypes are the nurturer, the protector, the chef, family homemaker, psychic, empath, healer, rescuer, tribe, and parent.

Leo Moon—A positive energy, a take-charge person, more patriarchal energy, yet seated in the feminine. Leo's feminine archetypes and traits are the divine child, the quiet leader, and a warm personality. Leos are inviting and magnanimous, extremely creative, forgiving, and loving.

Virgo Moon—A feminine energy. Virgo's feminine archetypes are healer, naturalist, and intuitive. In love they can be supportive, fair, wise, and ethical. They are picky, and do have a hard time expressing their emotions. Mother earth has a hard time expressing her emotions, and when she does, she yells through her earthquakes. This is what the Virgo does when exploding with a show of emotions.

Libra Moon—The love person. Venus is the natural ruler. Libra's feminine archetypes are the mediator, lover, companion, counselor, coach, diplomat, advocate, and Goddess. Libras have to be careful to avoid becoming love addicts because they have a hard time being single. They adore anything having to do with beauty, art, or music.

Scorpio Moon —A feminine sign. Scorpios can be emotional mushballs. Scorpio's feminine traits are empathy, having healing abilities, magical powers, and ability to spiritually uplift others. Scorpio's feminine archetypes are: guide, therapist, healer, psychic, and empath.

Sagittarius Moon —Sagittarius's energy is in tune with our mother, as outdoors in nature is a Sagittarian's favorite place to be. The feminine archetypes are the seeker, the intuitive, the visionary, the philosopher, the explorer, and the gypsy. Some Sagittarian feminine traits are ability to go with the flow and being optimistic.

Capricorn Moon —A patriarchal energy. Humanity is moving away from this type of energy. Some archetypes for this energy are strategist, disciplinarian, authority, tyrant, CEO, executive, bully. Not much femininity is to be found within this energy. Some of Capricorn's feminine traits are: being receptive, sensitive, and introverted, and a willingness to put one's feelings "on the shelf" and make huge sacrifices to "do one's duty."

Aquarius Moon—Associated with sending out into the world creativity and freedom. An Aquarius is loving and loyal, with an air of detachment. Sometimes this energy gives the appearance of emotional coolness. Aquarius's feminine archetypes are visionary, humanitarian, philanthropist, and prophet.

Pisces Moon—Pisces live for love. They love to cuddle and hug, and crave relationships. Some of Pisces' traits are shyness and sensitivity, which may cause them to hibernate. They long for union and a deep soul mate connection, but can be fickle. They are thin-skinned and fragile. They have to surround themselves with persons who honor their tender feelings and who are healthy. Some feminine archetypes are poet, artist, dreamer, and psychic.

To summarize these moon energies: we can look to see how each one affects in a different way the way we relate to our mother and each other through relationships. Looking at the energies of the moon helps us to evolve out of the patriarchal stronghold. Profound heart-opening is possible through understanding these basic feminine energies.

CHAPTER 8

Owning the Inner Masculine

For centuries, females were not allowed to assert themselves into the world. They carefully learned the role of supporter to their masculine partners. Along the way this model became zigzagged and skewed when the masculine began disconnecting and self-medicating. Consequently, the feminine in all her resourcefulness has learned to become successful at fulfilling more of her needs, thereby owning her own power.

The female owning her power feels disempowering to the male, even though he has disconnected and is mirroring disempowerment to the female. These energies are muddled. The goal during this time period is to blend both feminine and masculine, where the man accepts the masculine in the woman, the woman accepts the feminine in the man, the two get together, and the energies flow. The relationship is not based on need, want, or filling the wound. This becomes the divine feminine in relationships and creates the sacred union.

For the feminine to own her inner masculine takes a process of becoming at home with the ego, and gaining a true sense of personal strength and power. For the masculine to own his inner feminine is the same process of becoming aware of and comfortable with the ego of cultural spells about the masculine being feminine and owning that power as truth.

CHAPTER 9

Soul Love

The soul is encased deep with the physical body. It does not represent your family of origin or its traditions. However, through the lineage of the DNA, your soul does carry through each lifetime the origin of cultural traditions and wounds from people within that lineage who were traumatized, who shifted out of one belief into another, or who shut down their systems of functioning.

Since all this is going on with our soul we find the doorway of deep soul yearnings through the connection of love and our attraction of a mate. It is almost as though we have no control over the type of love we attract in our life. Yet, we do.

Because of the deep emotional connection that comes from intimacy followed by the pain of loss, parts of the soul split off and leave the body. It becomes much too painful to endure these feelings of loss. We have to clear the lineage, clear ourselves, because at this point our aura, the energy system surrounding the body, has become weak and punctured. All kinds of spirit attachments from the other unseen realm happen. These spirit attachments cause more harm and disconnection. It is a crazy cycle.

We have to take control and love our soul; stop all forms of self-medication, and step into prayer and meditation; take long walks in nature; express ourselves creatively; engage in soul retrieval, lineage clearing, clearing of self, home clearing, and clearing everyone in our realm.

Our souls have come in and out of bodies many times, and the process of growth for the soul is through the mirror of relationships. Even though parts of the soul have split off from loss and trauma due to relationship loss, the soul continues to learn the lessons intended in that lifetime.

The attraction dynamic and the push-pull factor of relating reinforce our love nature. All souls are love. It is the wound from current lifetimes, that causes the jolt, for making parts of the soul to leave. It is our job to confront that wound and to take all parts of our own soul back to our body so we can become whole.

Confronting the wound will cause us to look deep within and past the ego, and to listen to the still, small voice within us. The inner knowing, the inner intuition, the God within calls us forth to allow the feelings and pain of trauma to open and be listened to and heal.

We call into our life through the attraction factor another human to open that wound and look at the trauma and what caused the soul to split. The mirror factor is the initial attraction. This moment in the relationship is where we look deep within our soul to where the wounding happened. As intimacy develops, bonding takes place through the sexual connection, and the push-pull of "I want you—I don't want you," a power struggle develops. We have to stand in honesty. The truth heals.

Unfortunately, some souls cannot bear the pain the wound causes, so they make many different choices to numb the pain. Choosing to numb the pain can lead to addiction. Addiction causes more problems with disconnection between the two within the relationship, which then causes more soul split, and the soul disconnection with parts of the soul leaving the body. Eventually, the soul just leaves the body completely. The body is then dead. Twelve-step programs are really good at keeping the human mind focused and the soul within the body; they allow the wound to be felt and confronted, then released through the truth and reality of the situation.

As we practice soul love, or self love it propels us on the path of life that releases joy and peaceful feelings of serenity. Through serenity we are able to relax and let flow the natural course of life, and extend our relationship with God and all beings on the other side.

CHAPTER 10

What Love Is Not

L ove is not dependency, intensity, longing, yearning, or control. The feelings of longing and yearning are about lack, and are often mistaken for love. Intensity is the addict's high. We confuse intensity for love and use sex for the intensity, which numbs the shame and fear associated with both past and current sexual behavior. The love-avoidant male is emotionally dangerous in that he is incapable of love. The female tries to convince herself that sex must be the real thing, that sex must be love. In this type of scenario it does not matter whether it is within a same-sex union, because there is always a male and female in either type of union. The male of the union is usually the love-avoidant person, and the female of the union is usually the love addict.

A union of this type is a gift from God. These unions are teachers and healers sent to help us look deeply inside ourselves to heal the wound, and to direct us back to the source and to God. These relationships start with romantic love, and evolve through the mirror effect. The mirror is there to help us heal the anger, the rage, the shame, the guilt, and the pain of abuse perpetrated by another. We are driven to find our romantic partner, and to find our way back to God. We have contracts with these souls we call into our life. If we have been abused we are going to attract abusers. The abusers become our teachers. When we recognize this, we can say thank you to the people who have hurt us. The soul expands enormously in consciousness and compassion after healing.

We confuse feeling high with feeling happy. This is why addicts, when they go into treatment, are not allowed overeating, starving, vomiting, caffeine, sugar, antacids, or vitamins. These things can be used to temporarily medicate the feeling of loneliness and longing for companionship, numbing the pain of the wound. The wound is the separation from God, from source, from the Divine. To open the wound, one must feel the deep pain, so that the energetic cord and bond can be cut. Yes, it is possible to cut cords that keep us bound to another soul; but to finally be done with the hold one must feel the pain and then release it to the other realm, never to have a hold on one's soul again in any future lifetimes.

We are driven to find romantic love and a romantic partner because euphoric feelings of peace and oneness remind us there is a God in the universe. Then when we experience the crash and burn of rubber hitting the wound in the road of relating, we say ouch and jump ship. The trauma of relating, hurts, and we find it necessary to leave the situation. Sometimes we stay stuck in the mud of delusion and shame for years because the wound that drew us to the romantic partner closed right up the first time we felt the pain. We may feel God will disown us because we failed at marriage. Yet God does not care how many times we marry, or who, as long as we care about God and our relationship to God, the source, the Divine.

CHAPTER 11

Marriage or Union

Ceremony and marriage seal the bond between two souls. A union between two souls transpires in the unseen world before they agree to come together.

For some reason, humans have made marriage a business through the creation of legal words. Legalese can create agreements of entrapment. Since love never dies, why do we humans want to entrap others when the lesson is finished? Entrapment just causes wounds, soul splitting, soul dying, and escapist behaviors.

Marriage as we know it today is evolving. Traditional marriages based on the models of survival and security are illusionary and breaking apart. Our souls are telling us we want experience, not security, because our souls have come into this earth to evolve through experience. Marriage as society knows it today, has been an illusion. Becoming conscious of reasons to remain or to sever the marriage bond allows the souls to love from a deeper place.

Once we realize we are powerless to spend energy trying to control someone else other than ourselves, the illusion becomes visible. If the agreement at the level of the soul before coming to earth is to enter within a marriage based on societal rules and regulations, and then leaving through the legal system of divorce, then let it be.

If two souls contracted and knew each other through the spans of time, why would they need a legal marriage contract to say they are married? Shifting out of legal marriage into a place of sacred divorce is the new paradigm. The sacred divorce entails trusting the flow of schedule and timing, not necessarily legal divorce, allowing each to have their own life and way of living without daily living with the same household, meaning to live single while still legally married. Legal divorce costs money and there are many other fun things to spend money on instead of something that has already died. The part in the marriage vow that says "until death do you part" doesn't have to mean physical death; it can be the death of intimate relating that can part. Physical, emotional, financial, and spiritual parts can experience their own cycles of death within the traditional marriage cycle.

In the seen world, marriage is a place for partnership that receives blessings from family and society who accept the couple and send energetic blessings of good to the couple. The unseen realm weaves magic of light upon them. When they send positive thoughts, they send the light from those thoughts. The opposite happens when they send negative. Even in the unseen realm the negative thoughts have many repercussions. One reason marriage is so important to many people is because society accepts these unions, causing good, positive thoughts to surround the couple in both the seen and unseen worlds. However, marriage partnerships become corporations because of the signed legal words in a contract and a couple's purchase of joint assets. The true and real marriage between two souls happens with physical bonding and the alchemy of blending two energies.

CHAPTER 12

The Alchemy of Physical Intimacies

The bond that takes place in the realm of the unseen is the true marriage. The alchemy of the two souls coming together to bond with physical communication creates threads and cords in the unseen realm between the two bodies. These threads and cords keep people bound together until they are severed through ceremony or the work of a shaman or energy worker who works in the realm of the unseen.

If the two souls agree to come together fully using the alchemy of physical communion, this creates a marriage and bond in all realms of both the unseen and the seen. A type of communication is established between the two souls. Telepathic communication is not the only communication between them. They communicate with a knowing interchange of thoughts and ideas. One picks up on the other's thought within a nanosecond after the thought is released.

But if two souls don't agree to come together with full, physical communion, and one takes from that person without permission from the other, such as by rape, the bond in the unseen realm, through the threads and cords, still happens on levels of the chakras. The ramifications are still telepathic, and a knowing communication the female picks up from the male. When this telepathic communication is not acknowledged: such as, knowing why he will not communicate with her, then partial soul loss from her body is possible. With loss of the soul, many things happen in the realm of the unseen, such as tears in the human aura and negative spirit attachments. A human eye cannot see these threads and cords between the two bodies unless a person takes a step back to quiet centeredness and looks with a third eye into the realm of the unseen.

What happens between the two persons and bodies after the threads and cords have intertwined? The illusion from the mind that drew the male energy to the female energy is broken. Yet, in the unseen realm the cords and threads are much stronger in holding the bond between the two. With the feminine being the receiving energy, the natural nurturer, and the male withdrawing after these unseen bonds have been connected, the feminine can tap into any thoughts from his heart and his mind that the male puts out there.The power of the feminine is the feeling the male receives from the female; this feels scary for the wounded male—knowing the feminine sees him deep within and sees his unwillingness to look within to what caused the original wound.

The male disconnect from the feminine after those cords and threads have been established feels painful emotionally. The feminine knowing from within of the intuition knows what is transpiring with the male, yet the brain of the feminine sings a different tune of the heart. Because that intimate connection has been established, the feminine heart, feels deep emotional connection with the male. Since her brain, the mind, and heart are aligned, she is unable to rationalize the situation of male pulling away.

The receiving female suffers emotionally, in the heart, when the male stops talking after these cords and threads have been established. Remember, the feminine is the nurturing member: the mother, the one who makes the space feel safe, the sensualist, the holder of beauty, the patient and secure one, the guide, the teacher, the place where home and hearth happen and warm feelings abound, the empath, the healer, the listener, the Divine, the naturalist, the receiver of love, the natural companion, and the one with magical healing powers that allow the physical body to relax and go within. Yet because masculine energies have dominated as all-knowing, the feminine gets completely and radically discounted.

My Quiet Meditation and Talking to the Council

The shift begins as my soul travels into the unseen realm of the hidden, magical, energetic unwinding of negativity, when prayers are cast through the intention of words and thought in the positive realm of gratitude and acceptance. As my soul stands before the council of wisdom keepers to share my feelings of pain from this life, I feel nurturing of the Divine. The council listens. They pour gold through the top of my head as my body stays on earth. Looking down, the gold filters through the body, bringing it to a state of relaxation and peace. My thoughts say, "Holon of Ascension, the geometric shape Tom Kenyon teaches and surround me with the matrix, another geometric shape" as my soul slips back into the center of my body, centered and balanced. Being within the matrix and the Holon of Ascension allows me to look within the hidden realm while in my body, and to see why I am on earth, and the lesson to be. The negative dark beings from the unseen realm release their hold and their attachment to my body and aura. They fly away and I feel at peace. My mind is clear, allowing love and service to others on this path in earth's realm.

CHAPTER 13

The Original Wound

The original wound from the feminine began with the soul separating from the Divine to come live in a body on earth. Both the male and female are designed to love and nurture that new soul in the growing body, thereby balancing the original wound. The feminine gives love through nurturing, and the masculine gives love through provision and protection.

However, due to many generations of masculine rule and subsequent breakdown of the feminine love, nurturing the original wound has been forgotten. When this nurturing from the feminine and masculine is withheld from the developing baby, the wound grows deeper. The conscious mind cannot process the loss and disconnection from the divine source, God. If there is further trauma to that soul after being in the human body, then parts of the soul split off. Finding our way back to God and source begins the healing.

Love relationships provide a safe place to heal this original wound if both partners are active in nurturing themselves and each other. The feeling of bliss that comes from love is the same feeling the soul has while back home with the Divine, or God.

Through the different types of love attraction—erotic, karmic, spiritual, romantic, and family—our souls are drawn together to experience this divine feeling of bliss. Through this feeling of bliss, the tension in the body relaxes, the heart opens, and we return to the Divine, and to feeling the presence of God.

The scale of love balances through the energy of the feminine. The feminine of empathy, listening, giving, and nurturing balances the harsh energies of the masculine. Through the combination of feminine and masculine energies, the creative energy of the divine feminine flows to balance the scales of love for all of humanity.

CHAPTER 14

Affirmations of Love

Prayer in the Form of Invocation to Call in Love

I call into my life ardent love, earth love, eros love, sacred love, partnership love, and eloquent love, to feed all parts of my soul. I call into my life love that mends and heals all wounds from past lineage systems and the present moment of time. I call into my life eyes that seek the inner self, and that balance the feminine and masculine energies into natural flow. With your ardor, take me, and I take you. With your quest, find me, and I find you. With your determination and endurance, pull me through and help me climb, and I pull you through and help you climb. With your genius, enlighten me, and I enlighten you. With your fathomless depths, enchant me as I enchant you. With your healing touch, redeem me as I redeem you. With your shield, protect me as I protect you. With your actions, woo me. With your principles, win me. With your knowledge, intrigue me as I intrigue you. With your children, bless me as I bless you with children. With your strong arms gather me. With your light feet, dance with me. With *your willing heart, support me, and I serve you where we both serve the greater whole. And let it be so. Let it be so. Let it be so, as we send this prayer of invocation to the wind at all four corners of the earth, and allow love to return to ourselves whole, vulnerable and serving one another to the ends of time.*

—Kat Kemm

Mantra for Love

by Althea Gray
I am love.
I love me.
I am accepted.
I accept me.
I am safe.
I feel safe.

Chocolate Recipe

Author Unknown
1 tablespoon agave syrup
1 tablespoon cacao nibs
1 tablespoon cacao powder
2 tablespoons water
Stir and eat ... Yum!

Ask Your Heart

Stand up while holding an object you question on your heart chakra. Hold it in the middle of your breasts. Ask if this is the right thing to do. Do I need this? Am I supposed to do this? Am I supposed to buy this? Am I supposed to eat this?

If your body moves forward, the answer is yes. If your body moves backward, the answer is no.

Afterword

Through the process of experiencing many different types of love attraction, and finding an understanding of why my own long-term marriage shifted, I created Love Attraction Oracle Cards to help me understand the deeper issue mirrored back to me. The Oracle Cards have helped me when coming across a person I have an attraction to in understanding their teaching role in the love attraction. The Oracle Cards can be found on my website.

Katkemm.com